NOTE TO PARENTS

Sign language is a beautiful and expressive way to communicate which both children and adults will find intriguing. Sesame Street Sign Language ABC with Linda Bove is an exciting introduction to sign language. Photographs show Linda Bove demonstrating the sign for each letter of the alphabet and more than 75 useful words. Illustrations of the Sesame Street Muppets depict the words signed on that page. With the words in this book, children can have fun forming simple sentences in sign language.

ABOUT LINDA BOVE

Linda Bove is an actress who is deaf. She has been sharing her signing and theatrical talents with the television viewers of Sesame Street for many years as a cast member. She has also been seen in the movie Sesame Street Presents: Follow That Bird! and played the lead in the road show of Children of a Lesser God. She is also the author of Sesame Street Sign Language Fun, a book many children will want to go on to after this lively introduction.

A Random House PICTUREBACK®

Copyright © 1985 Children's Television Workshop. Sesame Street MUPPETS © Muppets, Inc. 1985. All rights reserved under International and Pan-American Copyright Conventions. ® Sesame Street and the Sesame Street sign are trademarks and service marks of the Children's Television Workshop. Published in the United States by Random House, Inc., New York, and simultaneously in Canada by Random House of Canada Limited, Toronto, in conjunction with the Children's Television Workshop.

Library of Congress Cataloging in Publication Data: Bove, Linda. Sesame Street sign language ABC with Linda Bove. SUMMARY: The residents of Sesame Street introduce the letters of the alphabet both in sign language and through pictures. 1. Sign language—Juvenile literature. 2. English language—Alphabet—Juvenile literature. [1. Alphabet. 2. Sign language] I. Shevett, Anita, ill. II. Shevett, Steve, ill. III. Cooke, Tom, ill. IV. Title. HV2480.B68 1985 419 [E] 85-1845 ISBN: 0-394-87516-8 (trade); 0-394-97516-2 (lib. bdg.)

Manufactured in the United States of America 11 12 13 14 15 16 17 18 19 20

I love you!

illustrated by Tom Cooke
photographs by Anita and Steve Shevett

FEATURING JIM HENSON'S SESAME STREET MUPPETS

Random House / Children's Television Workshop

Hello!

My name is Linda.

Follow me and learn

your A B C's!

Aa

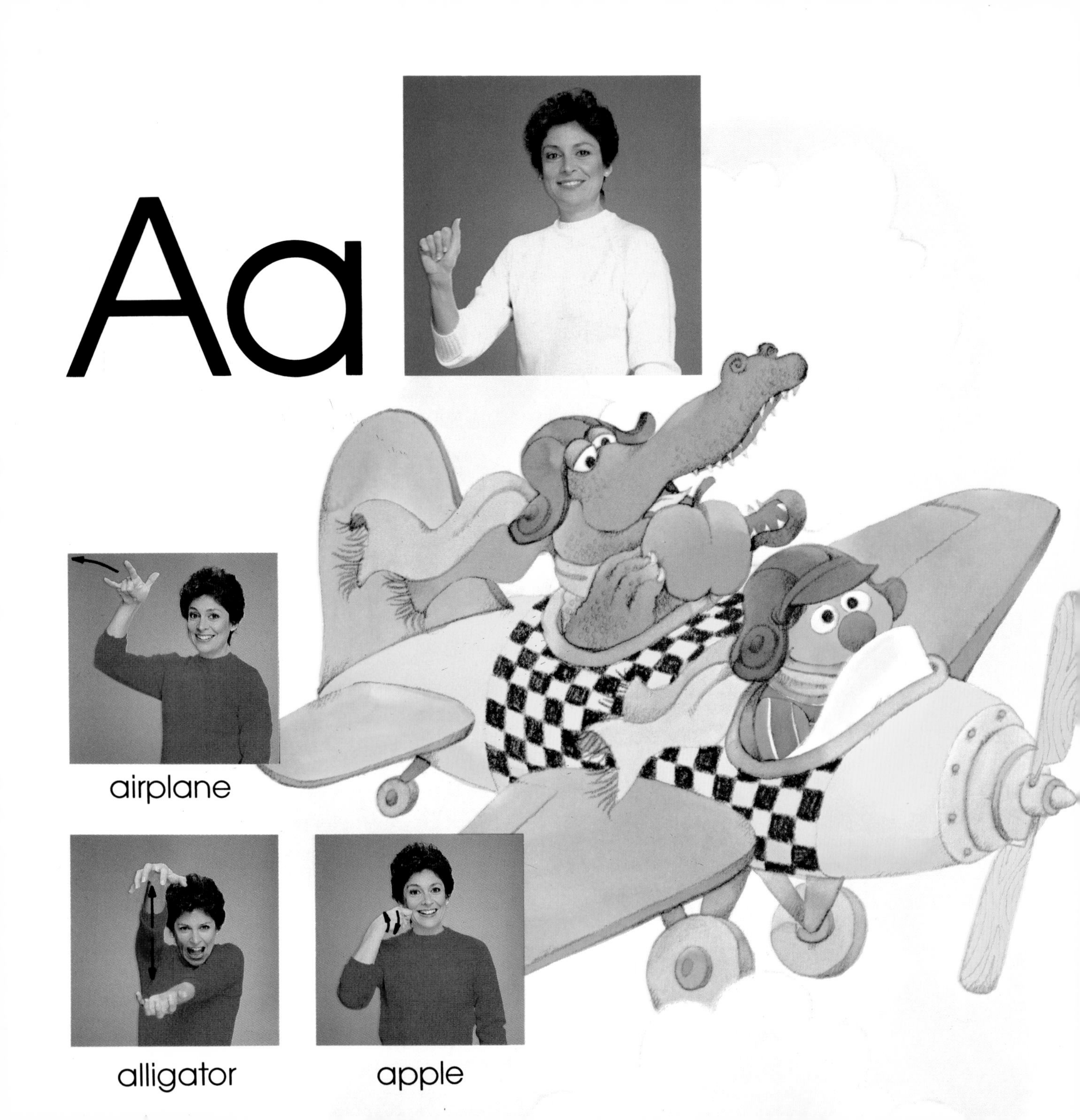

Bb
book
big
bird

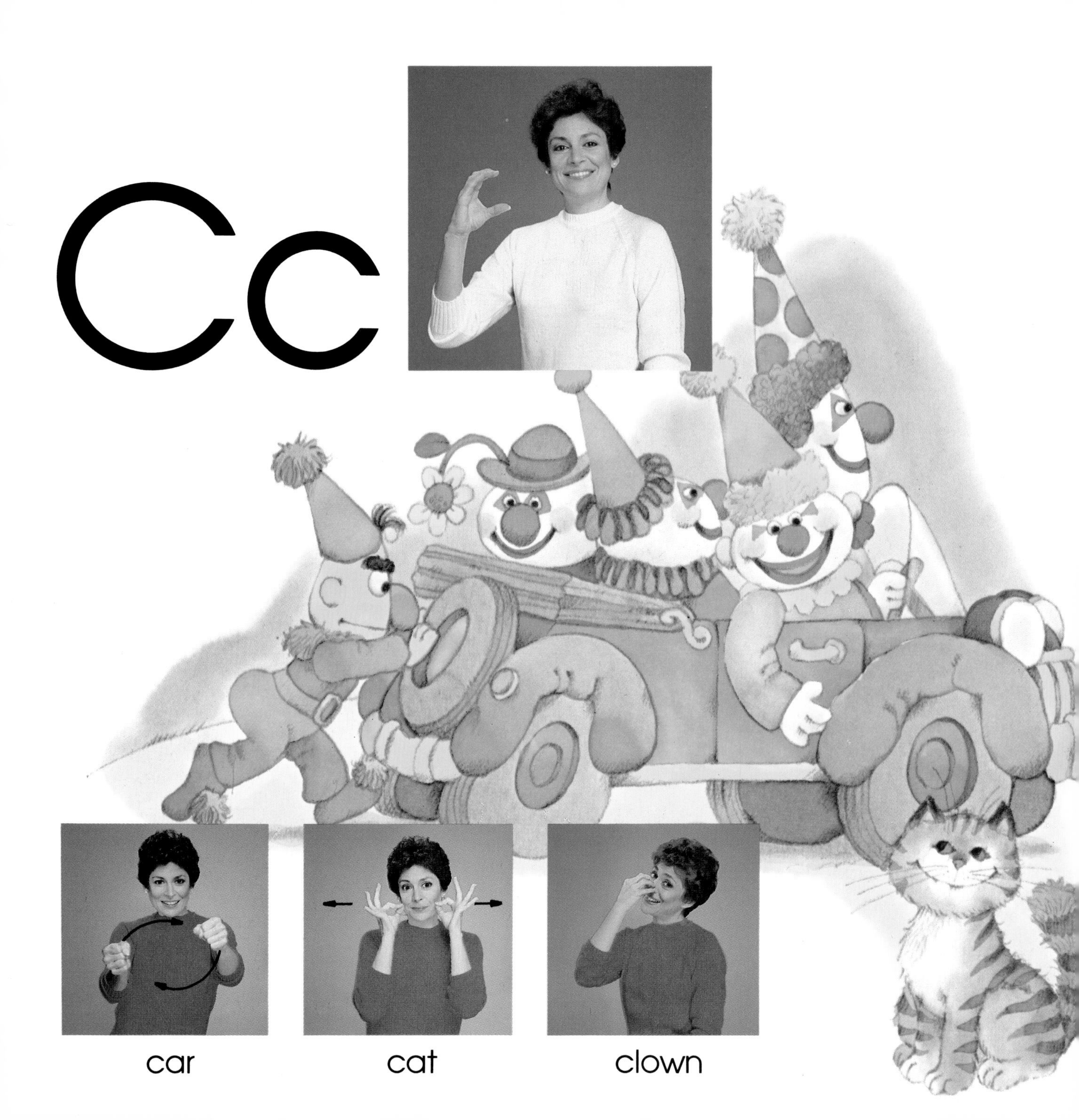
Cc
car
cat
clown

Dd
Where
is
my
duck?

Ee

elephant

eye

elevator

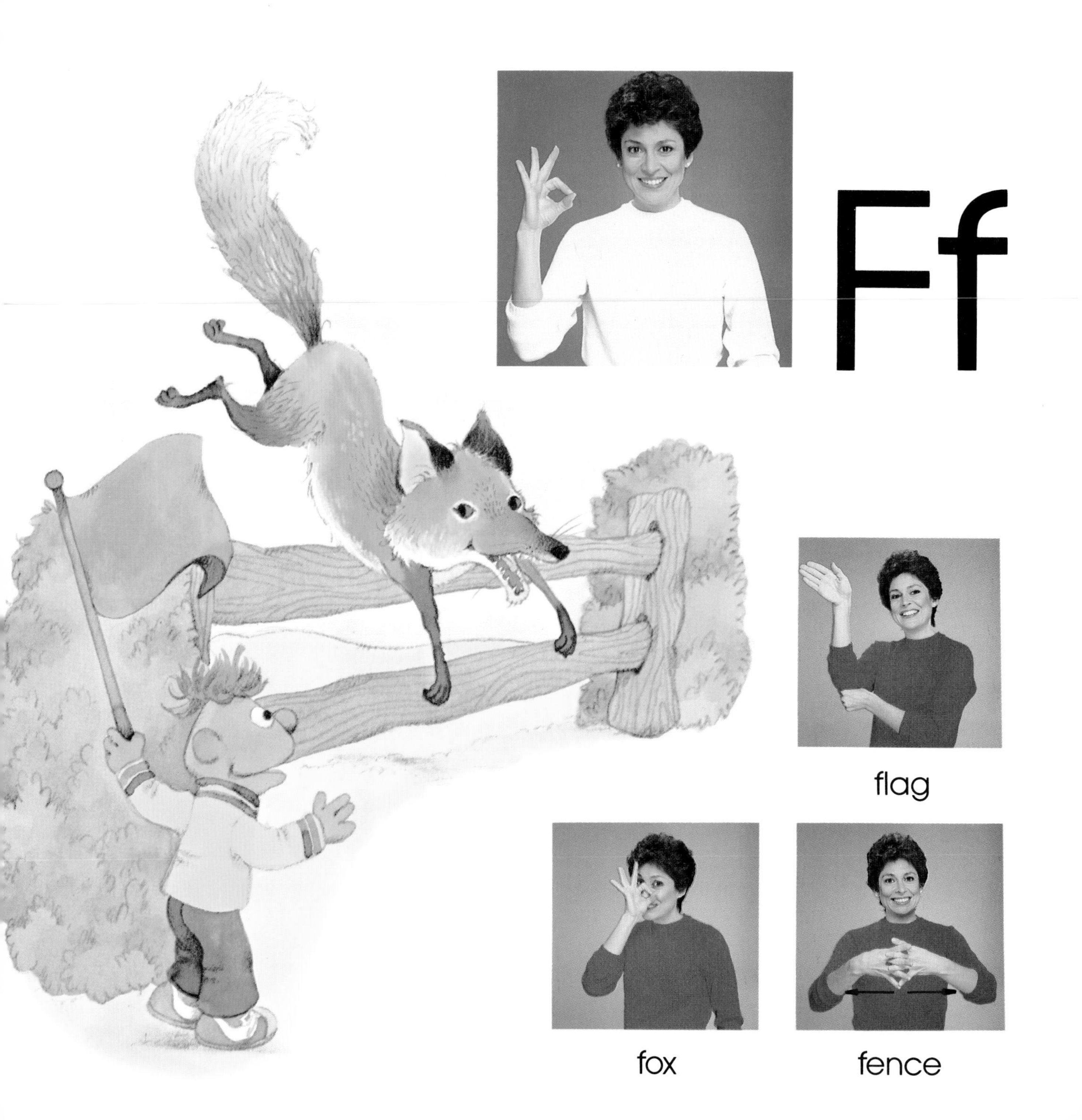
Ff
flag
fox
fence

Gg

girl

grouch

guitar

Happy birthday, hippopotamus!

Ii
I
love
ice cream.

jack-in-the-box

Kk
kangaroo
kite

Ll
2
1
ladder
lion
library

Mm

moon

monster

motorcycle

Nn

nose

nurse

Oo

Do not feed (the) octopus!

Pp
parrot
piano
pirate

Qq
Where
is
(the) queen?

Rr
rocket
rain
rainbow

Ss

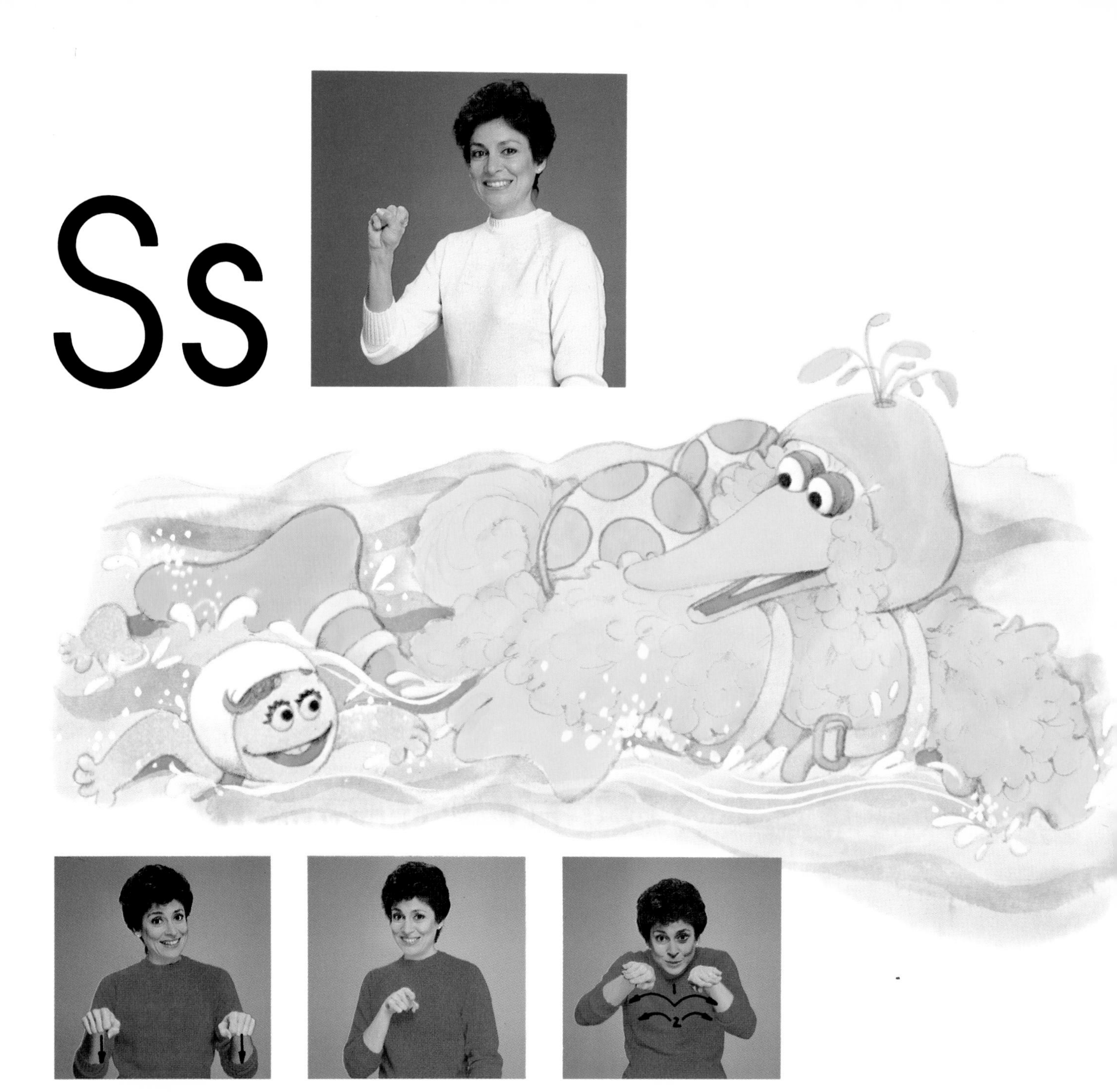

Can you swim?

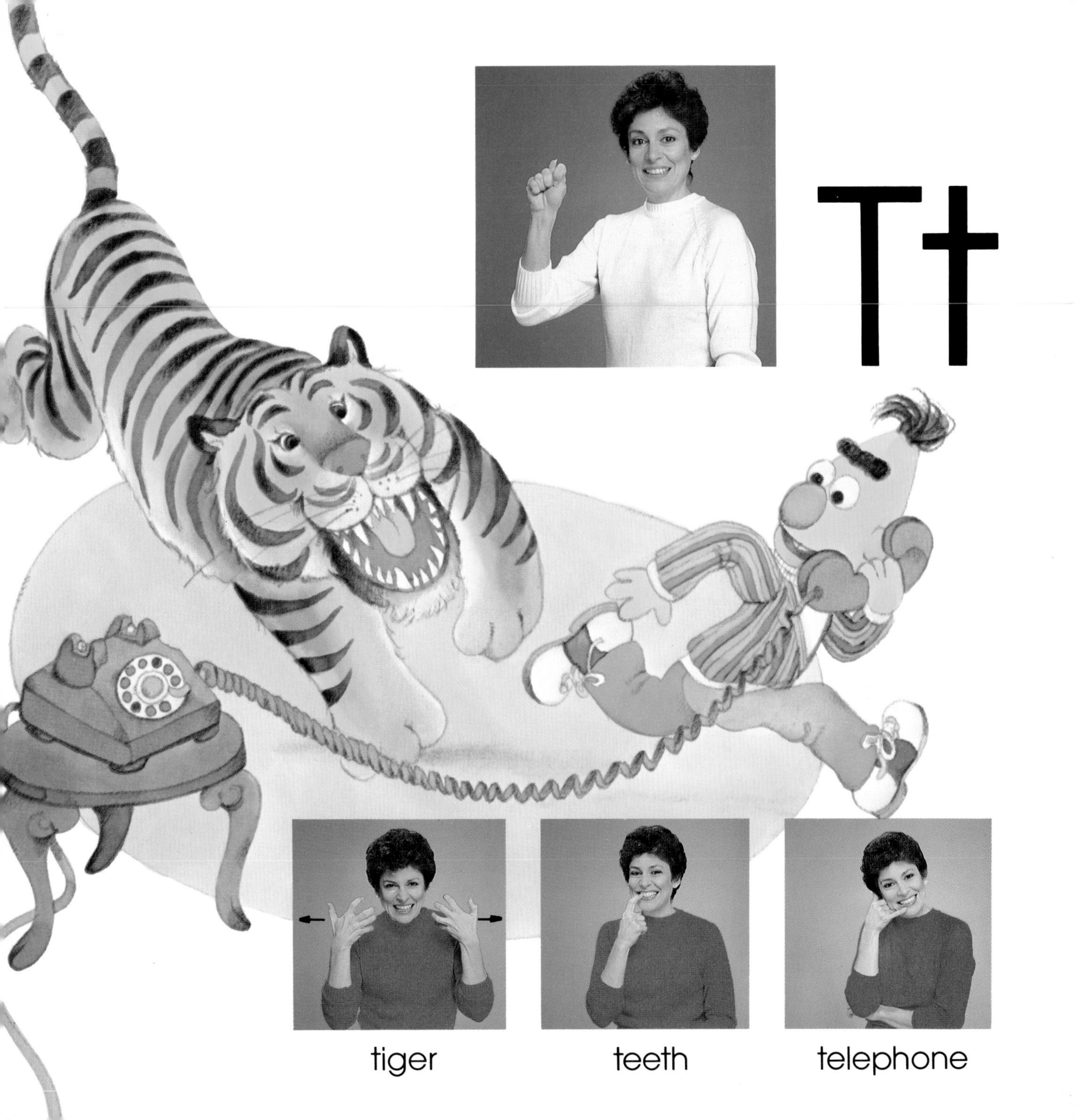
Tt
tiger
teeth
telephone

Uu
Come
under
my
umbrella.

Vv
I love you,
Mommy
Will
you
(be) my
valentine?

Who broke 
(the) window?

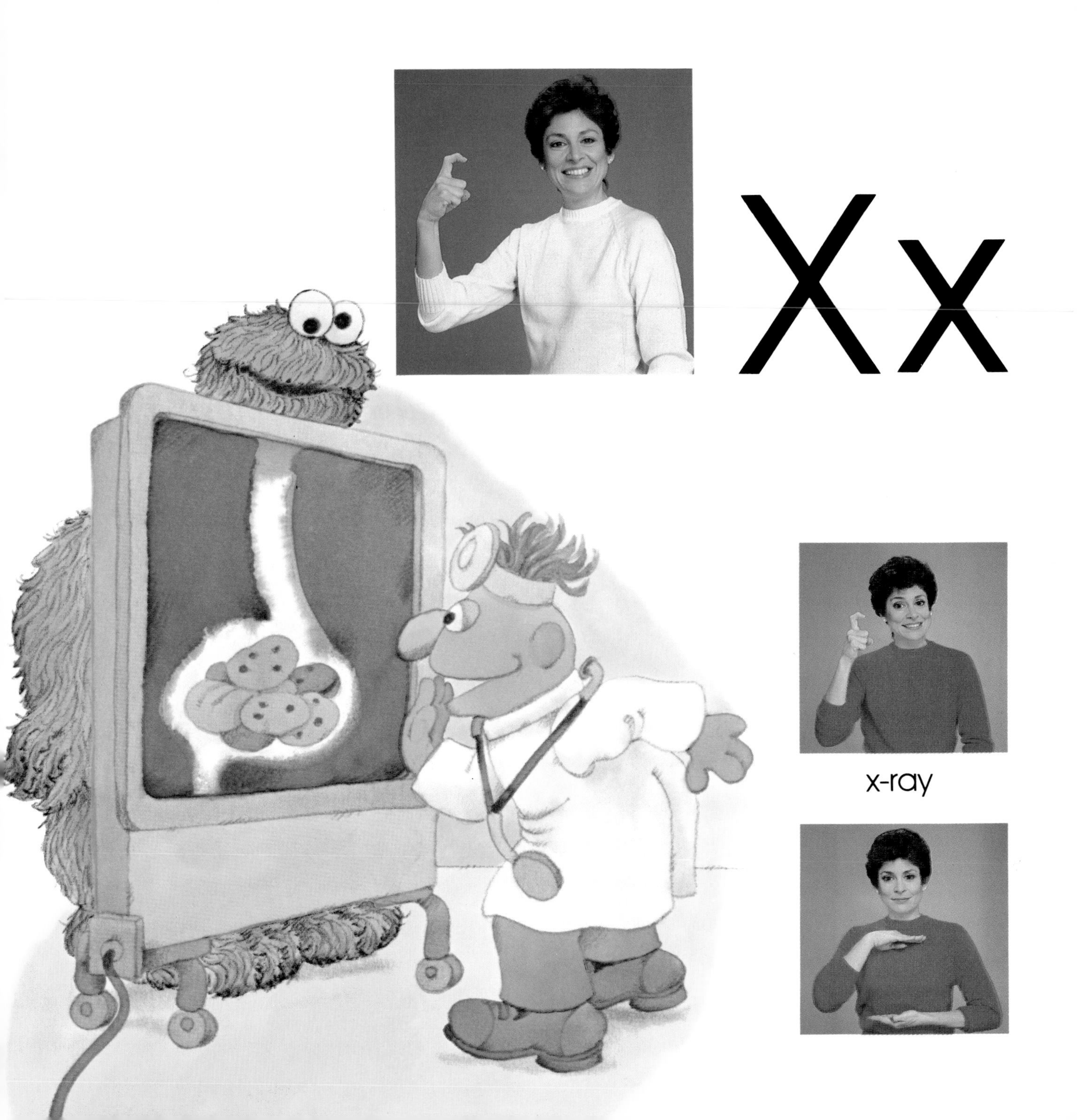
Xx
x-ray

Yy
yo-yo

Z
Zz
zebra

Now

I

know

my

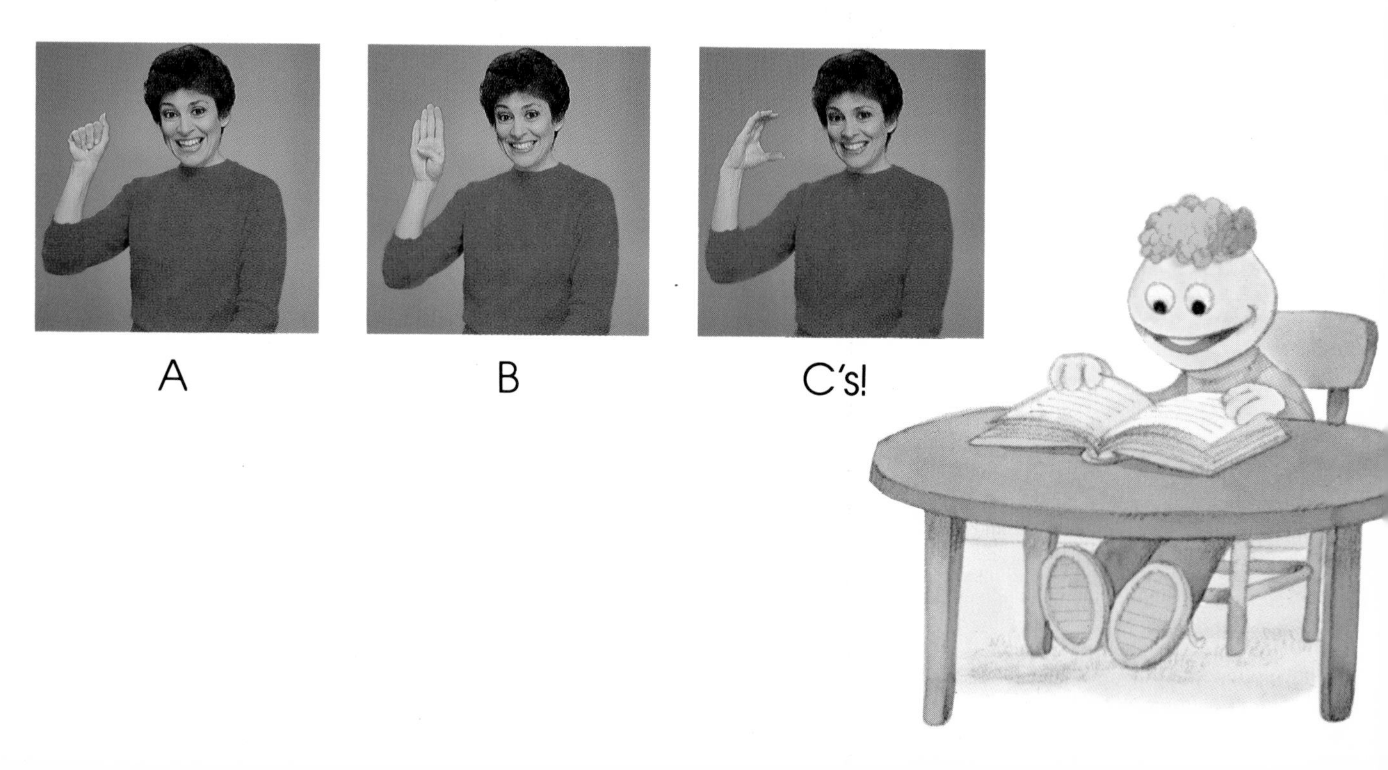

A

B

C's!